Swimming Lessons
and other poems

Maryalicia Post

Cyberwit.net
HIG 45 Kaushambi Kunj, Kalindipuram
Allahabad - 211011 (U.P.) India
http://www.cyberwit.net
Tel: +(91) 9415091004
E-mail: info@cyberwit.net

Contents

Definition of a poem:

A line of words
Cast by a poet
Caught by a stranger
Connecting them
Briefly
Before breaking

Market day

I didn't know that cows can weep
Feel fear, loss, anxiety
And now that I know
I wish I didn't..
So much to carry
All of us dumb beasts
On the way to market

Knowing better

I fail so many ways
Each day disappointing
The dog who wants another walk
A cat who prefers tuna
A grandchild who wants out
Of loving or being loved
And myself who's old enough
Not only to know
But to know better
Than to think it's over

Smile! That's great

All my photographs are happy
Sunlit days, gala nights,
Laughing children, smiling friends
No record of the other days
And nights
That were too dark for photographs
In failing light,
Some nights held stars
Others only tears

The root of the word courage is cor
– the Latin word for heart.

And so I think my heart is failing..
When it's courage that I lack
I will take the day on my tongue
A communion wafer
Dissolving
And pray
To look forward not back
To think of what I had
Not what I lost
That courage
Will settle round me
Like the trustful veil of youth

Looking for significance in heartbreak and finding none

Did it matter that my husband
closed our bedroom door in
my mother's house the day
we came home with our new baby
Did it matter that we wanted to be
alone as a family for the first time. Or
that my father put my husband out
for closing that door
And I went with him,
in my night dress cradling the baby
in my arms to his friend's house.
Later, we had our own door
And my father apologised
It was as if it never happened
My parents are gone now, and
my then-husband, and even the adult
the baby became. Did it matter? As much
as a breeze matters ruffling a field
of tall grass then leaving it still

Faith, like hope

Went out to see the roses blooming
Petulant heads
Won't show their faces
This cold morning
But in a crack in the pavement,
A bright-faced dandelion,
Reminds me once they were
The only flower in my world,
Picked and lain reverently on the altar
Of the local church before, as the saying has it,
I lost my faith. Each spring
When dandelions bloom
Yellow against grey
I remember it for a moment.

Swimming Lessons

Green bubbles in grass-green water
Bubbles with golden edges rise past
Nowhere to stand
Try not to swallow
Then father's arms lift me
To the edge of the pier
From which he tossed me
To teach me to swim
His black curls lie straight now
His white face whiter
Water running down
He tucks a towel round me
Hugging me dry.
Home on the trolley
Damp and silent
After the swimming lesson

Writer's Block

Poems wait in dark corners
At the edges of the day
Blow away at the first wisp
Of every-day light
A poem held hostage
Fights against itself
Let it escape
To grow stronger
And it may not come back

Morning in Dublin

Creamy dawn
Slides over the windowsill
Spills on the floor
Someone says 'is it raining?'
Someone answers 'probably'
Ah jaysus…..

The trouble with death

The trouble with death is that
If you don't know you're
Dead you can't enjoy it
Can't say.. today was the last day
For filing tax returns but hey they can't
Touch me now! How much
Better to miss a six-month
Checkup if you knew you'd never
Get another cavity anyway
Being dead means another day resting
In peace- not even knowing who held your
Hand before
'Not knowing' and how deeply
They miss you

Listen. Hear

This isn't how I thought old age
would be.. but then I hadn't thought of it at all
when I was young
Life was, it seemed to me, a feast
of food and laughter, friends
around a table in the sun.
But late you learn the sun goes in
friends called away, the laughter fades
And loss
becomes your daily bread.

5000 Piece Puzzle minus one

I start at the top - improbably blue
Sky and straight edges..
Then tree tops
Flurry of leaves. Buildings
People walking together,
Picture's complete
Except for the empty shape
Of you
Next to me
How can the picture be finished
With this piece missing?

Night flight

Do some birds fly at night?
I need to know
I'm looking for a metaphor
For thoughts that circle
In the dark
Dart into empty spaces
Lose their way
Try another
Til dawn comes
To fill the window with light

Godsend reading a postcard

It takes skill, to be a godsend
Putting life
Into postcards arriving.. look mom, they're in Spain..
That's a dancer. Yes I'll put it where you can see it
Take a bite now…
Spain. No, Austria was before that.
All right one more time, then eat something
It says 'lots of love'
Whoops.. don't worry….ready?
That's it….
Lots of love
————-from Spain.

Souvenir means 'to remember' in a language I no longer speak

In the airport
Checking in checking out
We bought souvenirs
-a jug marked Portugal
-a cup from Istanbul
-a Japanese fan
And do they remind me
 of these places?
No, that was very long ago
Now they remind me
That once we were young
And you were my world
A souvenir I unpack
Carefully
Each night before I sleep

Here is the script-
this is not just a reading

It was summer in the first act
When all the characters
Came on stage for the first time
Before the rain came
The wind swept away the decor,
Introduced the second act
The act in which I try and fail
To succeed
Here is where my character develops
Becomes strong enough to overcome
Adversity, making a happy ending
Plausible if not inevitable
Before rain turns to snowflakes
And the curtain comes down

Stating my ethnicity to whom it may concern

I am a member of the un-coloured race
Inaccurately called white
We're not really white..a kind of unlit beige
Like wartime rayon stockings folded
In a box
The women of our race 'make up'
For what nature failed to give us
Cheeks more pink, brows more black
Lips more red
We colour within the lines
As long as it makes any difference
Though some of us keep colouring
Much longer.
If someone tells us to stop
We may not hear them..

Recognise her?

Looking at old photos I turn away.
How sure of myself I was
How little I realised my world
Was temporary
No longer the person in the photo
I grab at memories as someone
Sliding downhill grabs for roots and branches
To slow their inevitable descent

Like wild horses

Words like wild horses
Sprint to the brink
Wheel around
Just when I fear
All's lost between us

Evening light

Evening light sifts through the branches
Hushing agitated leaves
Reminding me calm comes
Before the storm
And after, too.

Behind the Billboard

I was a child when the billboard went up near my house in Brooklyn. It was on a hill across the highway on bare earth known as 'waste ground'. The billboard advertised Ritz Crackers to homes like mine where penny pinching was an art form and Ritz crackers a visitation from another world.. What attracted me was not the hill or the billboard but the waste ground, the bare earth that stretched behind the billboard. Except for this patch, bare earth was unknown in Flatbush. Even our small backyard gardens were not bare. A dilapidated hydrangea would struggle on from year to year or a starved forsythia bush put out yellow distress flags in the spring. On the day I crossed that highway to explore bare earth I felt light with excitement, yet at first I was disappointed. Brown, flaky soil stretched out to a sagging fence not very far away. In the soil, some rocks, a few blown newspapers wedged against a wordless tree. But in a shaft of sunlight, up against the fence, there was a patch of green. I fell to my knees to see the small flowers blooming there. Like jewels spilled on a green carpet..Now I know they were violets... I couldn't name them. I didn't pick them. But I never forgot them. In another country in another life, I came upon a pink-flowered weed against a green fence. In memory of the violets, I took its picture.

Envol

In my chest
A bird flutters ready to fly away
If it must go may it be on a
Bright morning, dawn
Gilding its feathers,
As it soars
Swift as prayer into the blue sky